LEARNING TO LIVE SERIES

NAVPRESS

A MINISTRY OF THE NAVIGATORS

P.O. Box 6000, Colorado Springs, Colorado 80934

The Navigators is an international Christian organization. Jesus Christ gave His followers the Great Commission to go and make disciples (Matthew 28:19). The aim of The Navigators is to help fulfill that commission by multiplying laborers for Christ in every nation.

NavPress is the publishing ministry of The Navigators. NavPress publications are tools to help Christians grow. Although publications alone cannot make disciples or change lives, they can help believers learn biblical discipleship, and apply what they learn to their lives and ministries.

ISBN: 0-89109-062-2
10629

Scripture quotations are from the *Holy Bible: New International Version* (NIV). Copyright © 1973, 1978, 1984, International Bible Society. Used by permission of Zondervan Bible Publishers.

Printed in the United States of America

Contents

Author

The LEARNING TO LIVE series was written by Peter Dowse. Born in Great Britain, he has degrees from Cambridge University and London Bible College. Peter has been on staff with The Navigators since 1977. He led the student ministry at Sheffield University for several years, and now gives his time to writing and speaking.

Make the Most of This Bible Study

We live in a world of shifting values and conflicting viewpoints. Is it possible in the midst of this to know what is right and what is true? Yes it is! For God is true, and He has chosen to give us in the Bible a definitive expression of His own mind and will, His knowledge of reality, and His thoughts and plans for the world.

> *You will know the truth,*
> *and the truth will set you free.*
> (JOHN 8:32)

It is the aim of this Bible study series to introduce you to the joy and privilege of digging out that truth for yourself.

Personal Bible study is demanding. You will need to give it much time and serious endeavor. In this series, each lesson takes two to three hours to prepare. The rewards of personal Bible study, however, are great. You will surely discover this for yourself as you complete the books in this series.

Remember that Bible study is not merely an academic exercise. You will need to think, but don't forget that the Bible is God's Word. Pray before you start each lesson. Ask God to help you understand the truths and make you sensitive to what He wants to say to you through a particular lesson. Pray as you study, "Lord, what does this mean? How does this relate to me?" Praise Him when you discover something that excites you. The fruit of Bible study should not be just increased head knowledge; it should produce a deeper relationship with God and a lifestyle that is more honoring to Him.

If you can find others who are willing to put in the time to do personal preparation, you will find great value in meeting together to discuss each lesson. But don't let the absence of such a group deter you. Get into God's Word for yourself. You won't be disappointed.

When your words came, I ate them;
they were my joy and my heart's delight.
(JEREMIAH 15:16)

SOME EXPLANATIONS: The definitions given throughout this series are, of necessity, brief. More exhaustive definitions of the words can be found in any good Bible dictionary, for example, *The Illustrated Bible Dictionary*, published by Inter-Varsity Press.

Whenever the name of a person who has been quoted is followed by an asterisk, you will find information about that person in "Who's Who" on page 99.

Additional references are listed for some questions. They are optional references that you can use if you want to. For an example, see question 4 on page 14.

Each lesson has sections entitled "Ask Yourself." These do not require written responses, though you may want to write answers to the questions in a notebook. Each lesson also has a section entitled "For Further Study." These sections are optional.

The six books in the *Learning to Live* series can be done in any order, or you can follow this suggested sequence:

Clarifying Your Commitment
Living by His Grace
Living in the World
Disciplines of Living
Your Part in His Plan
Standing Firm

A Firm Foundation

The Apostle Paul declared to the leaders of the church in Ephesus, "I commit you to God and to the word of his grace, which can build you up" (Acts 20:32). As we consistently take in and apply biblical truth, we are being built up for eternity.

The lessons in this book will help us strengthen the foundation for our lives as Christians. We will clarify what the gospel is and what it means to be a Christian. We will consider the Person of Christ and His work on the cross. We will discover why we can be sure of our salvation.

We must never move away from these fundamental truths, but continue to deepen in our understanding and appreciation of them. One of the joys of studying Scripture is that as we grow in our relationship with God, so our understanding of His Word deepens. We look again at familiar passages and find new insights. We never finish reading the Bible!

What Is the Gospel?

The word *gospel* means "good news." The news is so good that the New Testament is alive with the stories of men and women bursting with a desire to pass the news on to others. Jesus Himself began His ministry by proclaiming the good news of God. "'The time has come,' He said. 'The kingdom of God is near. Repent and believe the good news!'" (see Matthew 4:17).

But what is the good news? A detailed study of the New Testament reveals great variety in the ways the early Christians communicated the gospel. However, certain truths are central.

The Book of Acts in the New Testament describes the beginning of the Christian Church. It describes how Jesus' early followers, led by the Holy Spirit, spread the Christian faith. In this lesson, we will examine their preaching, and seek to identify the central truths of the gospel. To make sure we have a balanced view, we will look at as many as possible of the gospel presentations in Acts. If you have time, read through the Book of Acts, marking each place the message is preached. The following questions will help you locate the gospel presentations.

Pause for Prayer
Before you start your study, be sure to pray. Ask God to help you understand the truths and to make you sensitive to what He is saying to you through this lesson.

They Preached a Person

1. The following verses summarize the message the early Christians preached. What was the message?

   Acts 8:35

   Acts 11:20

   Acts 28:31

2. To expand your understanding of what the apostles preached about Jesus, read each reference on page 12. List the basic facts communicated about Jesus in each passage. Then summarize the facts in three or four main points.

   (Several references are given for this question and for others in the book because it is important to accurately discover what the apostles said, and not simply project your own ideas onto a few isolated verses.)

MESSIAH: a Hebrew title, meaning "the anointed one," given to the Savior-King whose coming was promised by the Old Testament prophets. The Greek word translated "the Christ" has the same meaning.

Reference	Main facts about Jesus
Acts 2:22-36	
Acts 3:12-18	
Acts 4:8-12	
Acts 10:36-43	
Acts 13:26-41	
Acts 17:16-18	

Additional references in Acts: 4:33; 5:30-32; 5:42; 9:20-22; 17:18-34; 18:5; 18:27-28

"We must say that the good things the apostles announce in this gospel are simply Jesus." — ORIGEN*

ASK YOURSELF: a. How could I explain or amplify this statement: "The gospel is Jesus"? **b.** Looking over my summary of facts about Jesus, are there any aspects of His Person that could be more prominent in my thinking and witnessing?

Note: Jesus Christ is central to true understanding of the Christian message. The next lesson considers more fully the Person of Christ, with particular reference to His claims about Himself.

They Proclaimed a Gift

3. Read Acts 14:3. It describes the gospel as "the message of His grace." A similar expression occurs in Acts 20:24. What do you think it means? (The definition below may help.)

GRACE: God's undeserved favor; His unmerited love.

4. How do the early preachers describe what God offers to those who will respond to the gospel message?

Acts 2:38

Acts 3:19

Acts 13:38-39

Acts 15:8-9

Additional references in Acts: 5:31-32; 10:43-44

5. How does this offer represent the fulfillment of God's promises to His people in the Old Testament?

Jeremiah 31:31-34

Ezekiel 36:25-27

For Further Study
Other passages of the Bible amplify the teaching of Acts. What are some other things God gives us when we respond to the good news, according to these verses in John's gospel?

Reference	God's gift to us
1:12-13	
5:24	
6:35	

Reference	God's gift to us
7:37-39	
8:12	
10:10	
14:27	
15:5	

"Most religions tell you something you must do. This religion tells you of something God has done through Jesus on the cross."[1] — MICHAEL GREEN

ASK YOURSELF: a. In what ways does the gospel reveal God's generosity? **b.** How should the truths in this section affect my relationship with God?

Note: We never get away from the truth that our standing before God is based not on what we do, but on what God has done through Jesus on the cross. That theme is further developed in lesson 2 of *Guidelines for Growth*.

6. What response did the apostles ask for from those who heard their message about Jesus Christ?

Acts 2:37-38

Acts 16:29-34

Acts 20:21

Acts 26:19-20

Additional references in Acts: 3:19; 10:43; 13:38-39; 15:7-9

BAPTISM: In New Testament times, baptism was the seal on God's offer of forgiveness and the Spirit, and also on man's response to that offer in repentance and faith. In addition, baptism signified entry into the Christian community. Today, some churches consider it right to baptize the infant children of believers. Other churches reserve baptism for those who have come to a personal faith. You may want to ask one of the leaders in your church to explain from the Bible the position adopted by your church.

The definitions on page 18 have been derived by examining the literal meanings of the words, and by observing the use of these words in the Bible. Consider the definitions carefully and then answer questions 7 and 8.

REPENTANCE: a radical change of mind; a transformation of thought, attitude, outlook, and direction; a turning *from* sin, and a turning *to* God; not primarily or necessarily a *feeling* of being sorry, but a deliberate acknowledgment of guilt and the adoption of a new attitude.

FAITH: abandoning all trust in one's own resources; casting oneself unreservedly on the mercy of God; taking hold of the promises of God in Christ; not an unthinking leap in the dark, but a commitment based on evidence.

---

7. Read Acts 19:17-20. In what ways does the incident recorded here illustrate repentance?

---

8. Romans 4:18-25 describes an event in Abraham's life that illustrates the meaning of faith. Study this passage using the following questions.

   a. Where could Abraham not place his confidence?

   b. Where did he put his hope?

c. What immediate effect did his faith have?

d. How does the event in this passage relate to us?

e. How does this illustrate the meaning of faith for us?

ASK YOURSELF: a. Considering the definitions on page 18, have I responded to the gospel in repentance and faith? b. What should I do to make an open confession of my faith? Should I be baptized?

They Spoke with Concern

9. From the following references, what can you learn about the attitude the apostles had toward the people who heard their message?

Acts 2:40

Acts 17:16-17

Acts 26:28-29

---

10. In what way did this attitude affect the apostles?

Acts 4:18-20

Acts 5:40-42

---

11. What effect did their example have on others? Read Acts 8:1-4.

"I preached as never sure to preach again; and as a dying man to dying men." — RICHARD BAXTER*

> **ASK YOURSELF: a.** What motivated the apostles to be so courageous in their preaching? **b.** What can I learn from their attitude?

As you have prepared this lesson, you may have become aware that you have never truly responded to the Christian gospel. Perhaps you are not convinced that it is true, in which case you need to continue to investigate it. Or maybe you have never clearly understood the necessity of a personal response. If you would like guidance on how to make such a response, turn to page 93.

Stop, Think, and Pray

Look back over the study. What are one or two of the most important lessons you have learned (or relearned) about the gospel? Ask God to help you see what your response should be. Maybe you have grown in understanding, and you need to make sure you don't forget what you've discovered. Or maybe there is something specific you should do as a result of this study. Expressing your needed response in writing will help you follow it through.

Most important lesson

My response

One way to remember the truths you have studied is to choose key Bible verses and memorize them. You can select your own verses from the passages you study, or memorize the one suggested at the end of each lesson. (See page 97 for help in memorizing Scripture.)

Suggested memory verse for the question, What is the gospel?

Peter replied, "Repent and be baptized, every one of you, in the name of Jesus Christ so that your sins may be forgiven. And you will receive the gift of the Holy Spirit." (Acts 2:38)

NOTES: 1. Michael Green, *Evangelism: Now and Then* (Leicester, England: Inter-Varsity Press, 1982), page 73.

Who Is Jesus?

As we read the accounts in Acts of the early Christian preaching, we are struck by the fact that it all centers on the Person of Jesus Christ. The prime emphasis is not so much on what Jesus teaches, but on who He is. Because of who He is, the early Christians saw value and meaning and relevance in what He did. They believed the staggering truth that Jesus Christ, while true man, is also true God.

This belief has always been central to Christianity. But is it well-founded? Many people have suggested that it is the result of well-meaning but misguided reverence for a remarkable man. In this lesson, we will go back to the source. We will examine the eyewitness account of Jesus' life and teaching in the Gospel of John.

Pause for Prayer

Bible study is not merely an academic exercise. As you think about God's Word, be sure to turn to Him often in prayer. Why not begin this lesson by seeking His presence and help right now?

Jesus' Humanity

1. How is Jesus' humanness revealed in the verses listed on page 24?

John 4:6-7

John 11:33-36

John 19:28-34

---

2. The letter to the Hebrews focuses particularly upon the fact that Jesus was a human being, and upon the significance of this for us. What do the following verses teach about the importance of Jesus' humanity?

Hebrews 2:14-18

Hebrews 4:14-16

Hebrews 5:7-8

"Christ became what we are that He might make us what He is."
— ATHANASIUS*

> **ASK YOURSELF: a.** Why is it important to my salvation that
> Jesus was a man? **b.** How can this encourage me in my daily
> life?

Jesus' Confidence and Claims

3. Read the following verses. What do they tell us about Jesus'
view of Himself?

John 5:16-23

John 6:27-29

John 17:1-5, 24-26

Additional references in John: 2:13-16; 7:14-18; 8:42; 11:41-42; 13:3; 20:17

Additional evidence for Jesus' awareness of His unique relationship with His Father lies in Jesus' use of the Hebrew word *Abba* in prayer (see Mark 14:36). This is the intimate name a Jewish child might use for his daddy. To use it in prayer to God is without parallel in the entire Old Testament and in first-century Jewish prayers. Christians began to use the term because of the presence of the Spirit of Christ in their lives (Galatians 4:6). In John 20:17 Jesus Himself clearly distinguishes between His relationship with His Father as the unique Son of God and the disciples' relationship as adopted sons.

---

4. What does Jesus claim about Himself in the following passages?

John 10:30-39

John 14:9-11

In Jesus' teaching and in the rest of the New Testament there are direct claims that Jesus is equal with God. There are, however, many more indirect claims. This reflects the Jewish way of thinking. Jews are more inclined to express truth in terms of action than in philosophical statements. To say Jesus does what God alone can do is to the Jew a direct statement that Jesus is God, although to others it may sound indirect.

---

5. Compare the Old Testament and the New Testament verses listed below. In what ways can Jesus' statements be taken as indirect claims of His equality with God?

a. Compare Psalm 75:7 with John 5:22-23.

b. Compare Psalm 27:1 with John 8:12.

c. Compare Exodus 3:13-15 with John 8:58.

d. Compare Psalm 23:1 with John 10:11.

This is a good illustration of the principle that one of the best ways of developing accurate understanding of a Bible passage is to compare it with other passages. Many Bibles list cross-references in the margins or in footnotes to help you do this.

---

6. Look at the response of the apostles in Acts 10:25-26 and Acts 14:8-18 when people tried to worship them. Then look at Jesus' response to being worshiped in John 1:49-51 and John 20:28-29. What can you learn from the differing reactions?

Additional references in John concerning Jesus' response: 9:35-59; 13:13

"You must make your choice. Either this man was, and is, the Son of God: or else a madman or something worse. You can shut Him up for a fool, you can spit at Him and kill Him as a demon; or you can fall at His feet and call Him Lord and God. But let us not come with any patronizing nonsense about His being a great human teacher. He has not left that open to us. He did not intend to."[1] — C.S. LEWIS*

ASK YOURSELF: a. How have these passages strengthened my conviction that Jesus considers Himself to be God in human form? b. Which two or three key passages would I turn to in order to illustrate His confidence and claims?

For Further Study

Many other passages in the New Testament support this basic belief that Jesus is God. Read through the lists below and choose two or three favorite references to illustrate the fact that Jesus is God.

Direct statements
John 1:1-2
John 1:18
Colossians 1:19
Colossians 2:9-10
Titus 2:13
Hebrews 1:3
Hebrews 1:8
2 Peter 1:1

Indirect statements
Compare Genesis 1:1 with Colossians 1:15-17.
Compare Exodus 20:3 with Revelation 5:12.
Compare Ecclesiastes 12:14 with 2 Corinthians 5:10.
Compare Isaiah 42:8 with Romans 10:9.
Compare Isaiah 43:11 with Matthew 1:21-23.
Compare Isaiah 45:23-24 with Philippians 2:9-11.

There are also several passages in which Father, Son, and Holy Spirit are grouped together in a way that suggests that They are equally God. See, for example, Matthew 28:19, John 14:15-26, and 2 Corinthians 13:14.

Note: The fact that God, although One, is also a Trinity of three equal Persons is discussed in lesson 3 of the book entitled *Living by His Grace.*

Jesus' Teaching and Lifestyle

We cannot isolate Jesus' general teaching about life from His teaching about God. Nonetheless, the enduring quality of His moral teaching adds substance to His claims of being equal with God. So does the incomparable way His life displayed conformity to His own teaching.

---

7. What response did Jesus' teaching evoke in those who heard Him?

Mark 1:21-22

Mark 6:2

John 7:14-16

John 7:31-32, 45-47

"MOMMY, WHO'S THAT?"

8. According to the witnesses listed below, how did Jesus' behavior harmonize with His teaching?

John (John 1:14)

Peter (1 Peter 2:22)

Jesus Himself (John 8:29)

God the Father (Matthew 3:17)

The combined impact of Jesus' teaching and lifestyle continues to have great influence on believer and unbeliever alike. Consider the following quotations, both from vigorous opponents of Christianity.

"When this pre-eminent genius is combined with the qualities of probably the greatest moral reformer and martyr to that mission who ever existed upon earth, religion cannot be said to have made a bad choice in pitching upon this man as the ideal representative and guide of humanity; nor even now would it be easy, even for an unbeliever, to find a better translation of the rule of virtue from the abstract into the concrete than to endeavor to live so that Christ would approve of our life."[2]

—JOHN S. MILL (philosopher)

"It was reserved for Christianity to present to the world an ideal character which through all the changes of eighteen centuries has inspired the hearts of men with an impassioned love; has shown itself capable of acting on all ages, nations, temperaments and conditions; has been not only the highest pattern of virtue, but the strongest incentive to its practice. . . . The simple record of these three short years of active life has done more to regenerate and soften mankind than all the disquisitions of philosophers and all the exhortations of moralists."[3]

—WILLIAM LECKY (historian)

ASK YOURSELF: a. If Jesus' claims were false, either He knew it and deliberately lied, or He was sincerely deluded. After considering His teaching and lifestyle, what truths could I use to refute the claim that He was either a liar or a lunatic? **b.** What difference would it make to the Christian faith if Jesus were merely a man and not also God?

Jesus' Miracles and Resurrection

The New Testament does not encourage a faith based solely on miraculous signs. The miracles do, however, add weight to Jesus' claims. To simply dismiss them reflects a person's presuppositions; if we are convinced that miracles cannot happen, we will not accept the accounts. The eyewitness reports remain, however.

9. John's gospel records seven great "signs." These are miracles Jesus performed prior to His death. They are listed along with their references in the Gospel of John.

Turning water into wine (2:1-11)
Healing the official's son (4:46-54)
Healing the invalid at the pool (5:1-9)

Feeding the five thousand (6:1-13)
Walking on the water (6:16-21)
Healing the man blind from birth (9:1-7)
Raising Lazarus from the dead (11:1-44)

Choose one account to read and write down your impressions. What does the miracle reveal about Jesus?

---

10. What response did Jesus' signs, or miracles, generate?

John 2:11

John 11:45-48

Additional references in John: 3:2; 9:30-34

11. What particular sign did Jesus promise to those who did not believe? See John 2:18-22. Compare the passage with Matthew 12:38-40.

12. Read the account of the resurrection of Jesus in John 19:30-20:31. Which aspects of the story most impress you that the account is reliable, and that the resurrection of Jesus is a fact?

The other three gospels also climax with an account of Jesus rising from the dead. You might like to read and compare them: Matthew 27:50-28:20; Mark 15:37-16:8 (or 20); Luke 23:46-24:53. Each account is different. Commentators see this as the spontaneous descriptions of witnesses, not a contrived account of the event.

"As a lawyer, I have made a prolonged study of the evidences for [the resurrection of Jesus Christ]. To me the evidence is conclusive, and over and over again in the High Court I have secured the verdict on evidence not nearly so compelling. . . . The Gospel evidence for the resurrection . . . I accept unreservedly as the testimony of truthful men to facts they were able to substantiate."[4]
—SIR EDWARD CLARKE, former Queen's Counsel

The following items of evidence and a host of other detailed observations support the central truth: Christ was crucified, but now is risen!

- a genuine death
- a definite burial
- a huge stone
- a seal
- a military guard
- a missing body
- undisturbed grave-clothes
- reported appearances alive
- transformed disciples
- unconvincing alternative explanations

ASK YOURSELF: a. What evidence could I give to demonstrate that Jesus rose from the dead? **b.** How does Jesus' resurrection demonstrate the truth of His claims?

Stop, Think, and Pray

What are one or two of the most significant truths about Jesus Christ you have learned from this study? Perhaps you have grown more confident about who Jesus Christ is. For the times when doubts may come, make sure you can readily recall the reasons why you believe Him to be the Son of God. Focusing on Jesus may also have stirred you to think about your own life. Is there some adjustment that needs to be made in attitude or behavior? Take time to pray and ask God to show you what your response should be to the truths you have learned.

Most significant truth

My response

Suggested memory verse for the question, Who is Jesus?

Jesus answered, "I am the way and the truth and the life. No one comes to the Father except through me." (John 14:6)

NOTES: 1. C.S. Lewis, *Mere Christianity* (New York: Macmillan Publishing Company, Inc., 1943), page 56.
2. As quoted in *Evidence that Demands a Verdict*, by Josh McDowell (San Bernardino, California: Here's Life Publishers, 1979), page 105.
3. As quoted in *Evidence that Demands a Verdict*, page 105.
4. Sir Edward Clarke, as quoted in *Basic Christianity*, by John R.W. Stott (Leicester, England: InterVarsity Press, 1971), page 47.

Why the Cross?

It is a remarkable feature of the gospels that each one devotes considerable attention to the events surrounding the death of Christ. Clearly, the writers regarded Jesus' death on the cross and His subsequent resurrection as central to the good news they wanted to proclaim. Far from being a sad end to a splendid story, they saw the Cross as the focus and culmination of the life of Jesus Christ.

In this study, we will try to understand why they viewed it as such. We will look at Jesus' own references to His coming death, and also examine two of the pictures the Bible uses to explain the meaning of the Cross.

Pause for Prayer

It is easy to pay lip service to the need for prayer when studying the Bible. Yet God is waiting to help you understand His Book and to speak to you through it. Before you begin to study, be still and acknowledge His presence.

Christ and the Cross

Mark's gospel is the shortest continuous account of Jesus' life. Reading through it at one sitting gives a vivid impression of God's Son. His purposefulness is an outstanding feature of His life. He had come into the world to die. In this section, we will focus on the portions of Mark's gospel that illustrate this sense of purpose.

---

1. The turning point of Jesus' ministry comes when Peter recognizes and declares that Jesus is the Christ (Mark 8:29). Now Jesus can begin to explain to the disciples the nature of His mission. What can you learn from His teaching?

Mark 8:31-33

Mark 9:30-32

Mark 10:32-34

---

2. To what does Jesus compare the purpose of His death? (The definitions given on page 41 may help.)

Mark 10:45

Mark 14:22-24

RANSOM: In the Old Testament, the word *ransom* means the price paid for the release of slaves or prisoners of war. It is also the fine paid by someone who had inadvertently caused the death of another, a fine that averted the death penalty.

COVENANT: This is a promise God establishes by His own gracious initiative. It is a new deal offered to man. It is not a compromise agreement between God and man—something negotiated between equals.

---

3. What was Christ's attitude toward His death?

Mark 14:32-36

Mark 15:33-34

Throughout His life, Jesus was a most courageous Person. Yet He faced death with greater foreboding than many people less courageous than Himself. Martin Luther commented, "Never man feared death like this Man." On the cross Jesus seemed to experience a terrible sense of God-forsakenness.

Why was this so? The answer lies in the meaning of Christ's death. It was no ordinary death: It was a sin-bearing death. According to 2 Corinthians 5:21, "God made him who had no sin to be sin for us." In the following sections we will investigate what this means.

> **ASK YOURSELF:** What can I learn from Christ's attitude toward His death?

The Meaning of the Cross: The Law Court (Justification)

One of the most common New Testament expressions for explaining the meaning of the Cross is *justification*. Acts 13:38-39 pictures the Apostle Paul preaching in the synagogue at Antioch and saying, "Therefore, my brothers, I want you to know that through Jesus the forgiveness of sins is proclaimed to you. Through him everyone who believes is justified from everything you could not be justified from by the law of Moses." The imagery is that of the court of law, and Paul develops the picture in his letters, notably Romans. We will focus on that letter in this section.

---

4. In Romans 1:18-3:20, Paul brings into court before a righteous God the main segments of society: the amoral pagans, the moral Gentiles, and the Jews. (If you have time, read this passage and examine Paul's charges.) What does Paul conclude about the whole of mankind in Romans 3:9-20? (Compare those verses with Romans 3:23.)

"Nor is there any way out in terms of God's imply relaxing His law and ignoring man's law-breaking. The law is not some arbitrary series of demands which God chooses to lay upon the human conscience; at its heart it is nothing less than the demand of the character of God that man should conform to God's being and side with Him against all that threatens and opposes God. . . . Any infringement of the moral law amounts to a direct assault upon God. The moment we commit it, it becomes an integral part of that whole resistance movement which, in affirming His Godhead, He is bound to take account of and oppose."[1] — BRUCE MILNE

5. God in His righteousness cannot overlook sin, even though all mankind is guilty. Romans 3:21-26 presents Christ as the answer to this seemingly insoluble problem. Read through this passage several times and the definitions that follow. Then answer the questions.

RIGHTEOUSNESS (from God): In this context, this is fundamentally a legal term, referring to a status of being right with God.

THE LAW AND THE PROPHETS: the Old Testament.

JUSTIFIED: This is a legal term meaning "acquitted" or "declared righteous," the opposite of "condemned." Justifying is the judge's act. To be justified means "to get the verdict."

REDEMPTION: Basically the same meaning as *ransom* (see page 41).

ATONEMENT: This Old English word means literally "making at one." (*Atone* comes from *at* and *one*.) It points to the process of uniting those who are estranged.

a. How do we become righteous before God?

b. Why is this alternative to keeping the law necessary?

c. How is this alternative described?

d. How is it morally possible for a just God to acquit sinful people?

"Justification means . . . God's act of remitting the sins of guilty men and accounting them righteous freely, by His grace, through faith in Christ, on the ground, not of their own works, but of the representative law-keeping and redemptive blood-shedding of the Lord Jesus Christ on their behalf."[2]

6. According to the following verses, what are some implications for us of this way of justification?

Romans 3:27-28

Romans 5:1-2

Romans 8:31-39

ASK YOURSELF: a. The Bible says, "Man is destined to die once, and after that to face judgment" (Hebrews 9:27). If I were to die tonight and stand before God for judgment, how would I conduct my defense? b. If justification is a gift from God that I have received by faith, how should this gift affect my attitude toward life?

Note: The implications of justification are considered further in lesson 2 of the book entitled *Living by His Grace.*

The Meaning of the Cross: The Tabernacle (Cleansing)

The word *justification* explains the significance of the Cross in legal terms. The fundamental issue addressed is, How can a law-breaker avoid the condemnation of God, the righteous Judge? The glorious truth is that through Christ's death on the cross, the guilty person can be acquitted. This brings not merely freedom from condemnation, but also a new, right relationship with God.

The second picture of the meaning of the Cross is painted in religious terms. The question addressed is, How can an unworthy and unclean worshiper approach a pure and holy God? The Old Testament gives details of an elaborate system of animal sacrifice, presided over by specially-ordained priests, and conducted in a tabernacle built for the purpose. The first tabernacle was a portable tent. Later, a permanent Temple was built. The whole system was prescribed by God and pointed forward to the work of Christ. The letter to the Hebrews fully explains this picture of the meaning of the Cross.

---

7. Detailed instructions for the Old Testament sacrifices are found in Leviticus. Read chapter 16, which describes the Day of Atonement. Don't worry about the parts you don't understand, but make note of the things that impress you. To help you understand the passage, and the following references in Hebrews, a drawing of the tabernacle is given below.

THE TABERNACLE

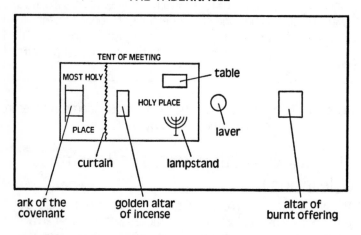

---

8. Hebrews 5:1-10 and 7:23-28 compare the Old Testament priests with Christ. What do you learn about Christ through that comparison?

9. The Old Testament priests enacted animal sacrifices. The New Testament presents Christ's death on the cross as a sacrifice of Himself. What do Hebrews 9:6-15 and 9:24-28 bring out about the quality of Christ's sacrifice? (Hebrews 10:1-18 also develops the thought, if you want to investigate further.)

10. According to Hebrews 4:14-16 and 10:19-23, what are some implications for us of the cleansing work of Christ?

A dramatic symbol of the effect of Christ's work is recorded in the gospels. At the moment of His death, the Temple curtain was torn in two from top to bottom. (See Matthew 27:51, Mark 15:38, and Luke 23:45.)

ASK YOURSELF: a. Is there anything I can do that will make me more acceptable in God's presence? b. How should the truths in this lesson affect the way I approach God in prayer and worship?

For Further Study
A deep understanding of the Cross requires an appreciation of the awfulness of sin. At its root, sin is rebellion against God. It is

refusing to allow our Creator to be our God; we determine, instead, to be independent. This self-assertion can manifest itself in many forms, and the Bible has a variety of references to the nature of sin.

In Psalm 51, King David confesses his sin to God. The psalm reveals something of the nature of sin, its extensive hold on us, and its effect. Read the psalm and use it to write a paragraph describing what sin is. Explain why God is so opposed to it and how the Cross of Christ meets the need David expresses.

The Cross in the Old Testament
The Old Testament gives many prophetic glimpses into the work of Christ on the cross. One of the most striking prophecies is Isaiah 52:13-53:12. Read through the passage and prayerfully consider its meaning.

11. What indications are there of the meaning of the Cross?

12. What can you learn from the passage about the cost to Christ of His work of atonement?

Bearing shame and scoffing rude,
In my place condemned He stood,
Sealed my pardon with His blood;
Hallelujah, What a Savior!
PHILIP BLISS
"'Man of Sorrows,' What a Name!"

ASK YOURSELF: How can this passage deepen my appreciation of Christ?

Stop, Think, and Pray

The Cross is at the very center of the Christian faith, so we should constantly be deepening in our understanding and appreciation of Christ's sacrifice. How has God spoken to you through this lesson? Perhaps your heart has been touched in seeing (again) what it cost Christ to bear our sin. Or perhaps one of the pictures of the Cross has focused your attention on the wonder of what Christ did for us. Certainly our response to these truths must be praise and thanksgiving. If you've not done so during the lesson, why not stop now and praise God.

A real understanding of the Cross also affects our attitudes and daily life. Ask God to show you any way in which your attitudes need to change and develop in the light of the truths you have been studying. Record your conclusions on the next page.

How God spoke to me about the Cross

The impact this should have on my life

Suggested memory verse for the question, Why the Cross?
 A helpful way to have the verses available for regular review is to write them on small cards that you can carry with you.

```
┌─────────────────────────────────────────┐
│                                          │
│  Why the Cross?              NIV         │
│                                          │
│  2 Corinthians 5:21                      │
│  God made him who had no sin             │
│  to be sin for us, so that in him        │
│  we might become the                     │
│  righteousness of God.                   │
│                    2 Corinthians 5:21    │
│                                          │
└─────────────────────────────────────────┘
```

NOTES: 1. Bruce Milne, *Know the Truth* (Leicester, England: InterVarsity Press, 1982), page 153.
 2. "Justification," *Illustrated Bible Dictionary* (Downers Grove, Illinois: InterVarsity Press, 1980), page 842.

What Is a Christian?

The word *Christian* occurs only three times in the New Testament. According to Acts 11:26, it originated in Antioch, probably as a nickname coined by those who observed the followers of Christ. The other two references (Acts 26:28 and 1 Peter 4:16) indicate that the name soon became widely used by the believers.

If the label was intended as an insult, it had no such effect. The believers found it most appropriate, for it focused attention on the Person of Christ.

Today, however, the word *Christian* is often emptied of its distinctive New Testament content. In this lesson, we will attempt to fill out the meaning of the word, particularly by examining other words and phrases used to describe the people called Christians.

A Christian Is a Child of God

The preceding lesson highlighted the tremendous fact that we can be right with God, the Judge and Holy Creator. We can be acquitted and cleansed. However, this truth, though great in itself, does not adequately convey the depth of relationship with God that is possible through Christ. The Bible's description of a Christian as a child of God makes one fact clear: It is a relationship of affection and intimacy.

Privilege

Read Galatians 3:26-4:7 and then consider the questions below. It is useful to know that in the ancient world, it was more common to adopt children of some age rather than infants.

1. According to Galatians 3:26-27, how do we become children of God? You might also read John 1:10-13.

2. What does Galatians 4:4-5 teach about how God has made this possible? Compare the verses with John 14:6.

3. What privileges do we receive when we are adopted as God's children? Look again at Galatians 3:26-4:7, along with 1 John 3:1.

Note: Although our focus throughout this lesson is on the individual, being a Christian is not a private matter. The picture of a Christian as a child of God implies that every other believer is a brother or sister. Galatians 3:28 makes the point. This important theme is developed in other lessons, especially lesson 6 in *Living by His Grace.*

Responsibility

Matthew 5-7 is often referred to as the Sermon on the Mount. In these chapters Jesus gives clear teaching on Christian living. The necessary background for this teaching is a recognition of God as our Father.

---

4. According to the following passages, how should a recognition that God is our Father affect our behavior?

Matthew 5:16

Matthew 5:44-45

Matthew 6:1-6,16-18

"OUCH!"

5. How should our understanding of God as our Father affect the way we pray?

Matthew 6:5-15

Matthew 7:7-11

6. In what ways should our responses to the daily pressures of life be different because God is our Father? Read Matthew 6:25-34.

Now summarize what you have learned from questions 1-6.

MY SUMMARY

A Christian is a child of God. This means

"If you want to judge how well a person understands Christianity, find out how much he makes of the thought of being God's child, and having God as his Father. If this is not the thought that prompts and controls his worship and prayers and his whole outlook on life, it means that he does not understand Christianity very well at all."[1] —JAMES I. PACKER

ASK YOURSELF: a. How often do I stop and thank God for adopting me into His family? **b.** How is the fact that God is my Father influencing my daily life?

For Further Study
Read Hebrews 12:1-13. What additional insights does this passage give into what it means to have God as our Father? How does God differ from human fathers?

A Christian Is a Believer
Believer is one of the first titles we find in the Book of Acts. For examples, see Acts 2:44, 4:32, 10:45, and 16:1.

7. Read Romans 3:21-28.
   a. What in this passage helps explain why Christians are called believers?

   b. Comparing the passage in Romans with Galatians 3:10-14, how would you explain the assertion that Christians are saved by faith *alone?*

   c. According to Romans 3:27-28, what is one major implication of this truth? Also consider Ephesians 2:8-9.

Living Faith

While faith alone brings salvation, the New Testament insists that true faith is never alone. It is a settled attitude of confidence in God that results in a changed lifestyle.

8. Hebrews 11 describes the way in which faith influenced the daily lives of men and women of God in the Old Testament.

   a. How is faith defined in verse 1?

   b. What remarkable statement is made in verse 6?

   c. Read through the list of things people did "by faith" (verses 4-12 and 17-38). Which ones stand out the most to you, and why?

9. Read Hebrews 12:1-3.

   a. How should the examples of the Old Testament characters recorded in Hebrews 11 encourage us to trust and follow Christ?

b. What parallel can you see between one of the steps of faith taken by these Old Testament characters and a step of faith you may need to take?

Now summarize what you have learned in questions 7-9.

MY SUMMARY

A Christian is a believer. This means

"The true living faith, which the Holy Spirit instills in the heart, simply cannot be idle." — MARTIN LUTHER*

ASK YOURSELF: a. What are some specific actions in my life that were prompted by faith? b. What am I currently trusting God to do in my life?

Note: The place of faith in daily life is considered in greater depth in lesson 2 of *Disciplines of Living*.

A Christian Is a Disciple

Disciple is the term used most frequently in Acts for followers of Christ. According to Acts 11:26, "The disciples were first called Christians at Antioch." The word *disciple* has the root meaning of "learner." But the disciple of Christ is more than a pupil. He or she actively seeks to follow the Master. The invitation to follow is a personal one from the Master. In this section we will examine the meaning of discipleship using Luke's gospel.

Considered Commitment

10. In the following passages, how does Jesus describe the commitment expected of His disciples?

    Luke 9:23-26

    Luke 14:25-33 (Referring to Matthew 10:37 might help you understand verse 26.)

11. What reassurance does Jesus give in Luke 18:28-30?

12. According to the following verses, how should this commitment to Jesus be demonstrated?

Luke 6:46-49

Luke 10:38-42

Additional references in Luke: 8:19-21; 11:27-28

Now summarize what you have learned in questions 10-12.

MY SUMMARY

A Christian is a disciple of Jesus Christ. This means

"Christianity is the total commitment of all I know of me to all I know of Jesus Christ." — WILLIAM TEMPLE*

ASK YOURSELF: **a.** Do I understand and accept the truth that to be a Christian means giving Jesus Christ first place in my life and living the rest of my life as His disciple? **b.** In what way is Jesus calling me to obey His Word today?

Note: The theme of obedience is also considered in *Disciplines of Living*.

Stop, Think, and Pray

You might find it helpful to look over your three summaries. Look for ways God has strengthened your understanding. Be specific as you write down your responses.

Main truth I have learned (or relearned)

The response God is asking me to make

The practical action I should take

Suggested memory verse for the question, What is a Christian?

Yet to all who received him, to those who believed in his name, he gave the right to become children of God. (John 1:12)

NOTES: 1. J.I. Packer, *Knowing God* (Downers Grove, Illinois: InterVarsity Press, 1973), page 182.

Can We Be Sure?

Assurance of our salvation involves a conviction that the promise of salvation in Christ is true. It also involves a confidence that we have been saved and will be kept safe for eternity. This second dimension raises questions for some people. Can we be sure that our sins are forgiven? Can we be certain that we will go to Heaven? Can we know without a doubt that we are right with God? If we are sure, are such assurances proud presumption?

The Bible does contain clear warnings against the sort of misplaced assurance that makes people smug and complacent. On the other hand, the Christians portrayed in the New Testament have a clear and happy certainty about their salvation. Moreover, far from discouraging such confidence, the apostles seem eager to strengthen it and promote it.

If such a happy certainty is possible, what is its source? Where can we find the foundation for a right assurance? We will address these questions in this lesson. We will also look briefly at some possible causes of doubt.

Pause for Prayer

Don't forget to pray before you begin, and then maintain an attitude of prayer as you consider the various passages and their application to your life.

The Assurance of the Apostles

1. What can you learn from the following two passages about the confidence the apostles had both for themselves and their hearers?

Romans 5:1-2

1 John 3:1-3

HOPE: The word translated "hope" in the New Testament means a confident expectation of a future event. It does not carry the element of uncertainty conveyed by contemporary usage.

Assurance from Understanding God's Word to Us

Ultimately, it is the Holy Spirit who assures us of our salvation. However, He does not work independently of God's Word. Knowing and understanding what God says and does leads us to assurance. Paul's prayer for the Christians in Colossians 2:2 is that they might have "a wealth of assurance, such as understanding brings."[1] In this section we will pursue that understanding.

The Promises of Jesus

2. Listed on page 67 are references for three of Jesus' promises. Think them over carefully and prayerfully. Take time to

emphasize key words and phrases. Then explain how each promise can strengthen your assurance.

John 5:24

John 6:37-40

John 10:27-30

The confidence we place in a promise depends on the known integrity and reliability of the speaker. In the Victorian language of missionary David Livingstone, any promise Jesus makes is "the word of a gentleman of the most strict and sacred honor. He cannot break his word."

The Work of Christ

3. According to Romans 5:6-11, how does Christ's death on the cross guarantee our ultimate salvation?

4. Another very helpful passage on the work of Christ is Hebrews 10:11-23. Read through it and then answer the following questions.

   a. According to verses 11-14, what major reason do we have for being assured of our salvation?

   b. What further explanation do you find in verses 15-18?

   c. What additional assurance is introduced in verse 21? Also refer to Hebrews 7:23-25.

   d. What should this confidence enable us to do?

No condemnation now I dread,
Jesus and all in him is mine!
Alive in him, my living head,
And clothed in righteousness divine.
Bold I approach the eternal throne,
And claim the crown, through Christ my own.
CHARLES WESLEY*
"And Can It Be?"

The Character of God

5. Romans 8:31-39 also reminds us of the finished work of Christ, and that Jesus Himself is at the right hand of God interceding for us. In addition, it draws attention to the character of God.

   a. What does the passage tell us about God's attitude toward us?

   b. How can this knowledge of what God is like deepen our assurance?

"Christ's death is not only the ground of our redemption, but the pledge and proof of God's longing and determination that we should enter into its benefits. . . . If God has gone to such extreme lengths to save us, we may be sure that He has provided all that is necessary for its effective application and satisfactory conclusion."[2] — MICHAEL GRIFFITHS

The Purposes of God

6. We are unable to fully understand the purposes of God in the world. However, to help and encourage us, He does reveal something of what He is doing. How can the following passages strengthen our assurance of salvation?

Romans 8:28-30

1 Corinthians 1:8-9

Additional references: Ephesians 1:11-14; 1 Peter 1:3-5

The relationship between God's sovereign purposes and man's free will is beyond our ability to understand. Both are clearly taught in the Bible, so in some mysterious way, God is able to organize things without setting aside one or the other. Our difficulty in understanding how they can be combined should not stop us from believing in both.

"I believe in the doctrine of election, because I am quite sure that if God had not chosen me I would never have chosen him; and I am sure he chose me before I was born, or else he would never have chosen me afterward." — CHARLES H. SPURGEON*

In this section we have considered four great foundations for assurance of salvation. Summarize what you have learned about each one.

The promises of Jesus

The work of Christ

The character of God

ASK YOURSELF: **a.** Does my assurance of salvation place sufficient emphasis on these foundational truths? **b.** Is there any way in which I could strengthen my understanding of them?

Assurance from Recognizing God's Work in Us
The Witness of the Spirit

7. According to Ephesians 1:13-14, what is the ultimate guarantee of our salvation?

8. Read Romans 8:15-16. What will be one effect of the presence of the Spirit in our lives?

"The testimony of the Spirit is an inward impression of the soul whereby the Spirit of God directly witnesses to my spirit that I am a child of God, that Jesus Christ has loved me and given Himself for me: and that all my sins are blotted out, and I, even I, am reconciled to God." —JOHN WESLEY*

The Tests of the Spirit

While an inward conviction of being a child of God is a joyful thing, it is a very subjective matter. Such an inward conviction can be claimed by those whose lives give no indication that they are genuine Christians.

First John focuses on the subject of assurance of salvation. In particular, it addresses the issue described above. To counter the claims of false teachers, it specifies certain objective tests to determine the presence of the Spirit.

9. As presented in the following references in 1 John, what should be evident in the lives of genuine Christians? Read through each group of references and then summarize them with one key point.

   a. Read these references in the context of 1 John 1:8-2:2. A Christian is certainly not without sin. We need to distinguish between one who is striving to be holy yet falling into sin, and one who is willfully continuing in wrong ways.

      1 John 2:3-6; 2:29; 3:6-9; 3:24; 5:3-4; 5:18. Key point:

b. 1 John 2:9-10; 3:10; 3:14; 4:7-8; 4:16. Key point:

c. 1 John 2:23-24; 4:2-3; 4:15; 5:1; 5:10. Key point:

As well as exposing false claims of a Christian experience, these objective tests are reassuring when our inner confidence of salvation is elusive. On the other hand, the tests can be disheartening to some sensitive Christians. For such people, 1 John 3:19-20 is relevant; God's evaluation of our life is far more objective than our evaluation is. Even if we can see nothing positive, God will not forget or ignore the evidence of genuine new life. He knows everything.

---

10. Although John is concerned about exposing false claims of a Christian experience, he does not undermine genuine assurance. What was one of his main reasons for writing, according to 1 John 5:13?

According to 1 John, to become a Christian is:

> to have come to know Him (2:3).
> to be in the light (2:9-11).
> to have passed from death to life (3:14).
> to have been born of God (4:7).
> to have eternal life (5:11-12).

These phrases do not suggest an ongoing process with a doubtful conclusion, but a decisive past event with continuing implications. The terminology suggests that being a Christian is something about which one can expect to be sure.

For Further Study

Read quickly through the entire letter of 1 John. How often does the phrase *we know* occur? What does this teach about assurance of salvation?

ASK YOURSELF: How could the truths in this section reinforce my assurance of salvation?

Dealing with Doubt

As we have seen in 1 John, it is possible to have a false assurance of salvation. To the person who affirms faith in Christ, but over a period of time demonstrates no commitment to a new life, the Bible offers no assurance. On the contrary, it challenges such complacency: "Examine yourselves to see whether you are in the faith" (2 Corinthians 13:5).

In addition, we must not confuse assurance of salvation with salvation itself. Some who are genuinely saved may never have a clear confidence of that. The reasons for this vary; for some it may be ignorance, while for others it may reflect psychological or emotional weakness. Whatever the reason, their lack of assurance cannot take away their ultimate salvation. Lack of assurance can, however, detract from their present enjoyment of salvation. God would have it otherwise; He desires that each one of His children be assured of their adoption into His eternal family.

All of us, however, are subject to doubt at some time or another. It is natural and, indeed, important in helping us distinguish truth from error. If we are to maintain a healthy assurance of faith, we need to learn to handle doubts. In this section we will look briefly at two common causes of doubt.

Doubt from Having Inadequate Reasons for Faith

11. Read Luke 1:1-4.

    a. What was Luke's purpose in writing his gospel?

    b. What facts convince you that Christianity is true?

We all come across issues to which we cannot find answers. And we all experience events in our own lives or in the lives of others that we cannot understand. If our faith is to survive these challenges, we need to know why we nonetheless believe in God. If we can believe in Him, then we can trust that He has the answers and knows the reasons.

If our faith is simply based on the assertion that Christianity works, it will not be able to survive those agonizing periods when it appears most certainly not to work. Also, we will not have much to say to the person who appears to have another working philosophy of life. We can prepare ourselves now by establishing convictions about the fundamental Christian beliefs so that when events drive us to doubt, we have reasons for faith.

Doubt from Adopting a False Perspective

12. Read Psalm 73.

   a. What caused the psalmist to doubt?

   b. How did he get his perspective straight again?

"Faith . . . is the art of holding on to things your reason has once accepted, in spite of your changing moods." — C.S. LEWIS*

Stop, Think, and Pray

Look over the various "Ask Yourself" questions. What has God been speaking to you about on this issue of assurance of salvation? Perhaps there is something you have learned and need to remember. How are you going to make sure you do? Or perhaps there's something specific you should do. Commit your responses to writing to make them specific.

What has God been speaking to me about?

What response do I need to make?

How am I going to go about it?

Suggested memory verse for the question, Can we be sure?

I tell you the truth, whoever hears my word and believes him who sent me has eternal life and will not be condemned; he has crossed over from death to life. (John 5:24)

NOTES: 1. William F. Arndt and F. Wilbur Gingrich, *A Greek-English Lexicon of the New Testament* (Chicago: The University of Chicago Press, 1957), page 676.
2. Michael Griffiths, *Christian Assurance* (Leicester, England: InterVarsity Press, 1971), page 32.

What Now?

To become a Christian is to begin a new life. A "born-again" Christian who shows no signs of life or growth is a contradiction in terms. Already in these lessons we have begun to notice ways in which a Christian's new life should be worked out in daily experience.

As we pursue the theme in this lesson, we will continue to look back to what God has already done for us. It is of great importance that we keep this in view because it is the foundation for all growth. We must not fall into the trap of viewing Christian growth as a do-it-yourself moral reformation. On the contrary, it is allowing the new life God has given us in Christ to flourish. It is giving the Spirit of Christ freedom to pervade us and transform us.

In this lesson we will undertake an in-depth study of just two verses: Colossians 2:6 and 7. When concentrating on small portions of the Bible, it is important to see them in their context. Begin by reading Colossians 2:1-15, or if you have time, all four chapters of the letter. Then prayerfully focus on verses 6 and 7. Think about the meanings of the various phrases. Emphasize different words. Reflect upon the various pictures used to illustrate the points. The following questions should help you explore these verses more fully by introducing other references and suggesting practical implications.

So Then, Just as You Received Christ Jesus as Lord, Continue to Live in Him

This section draws on knowledge you have gained from the earlier lessons in this book, particularly lessons 1 and 4. In answering the questions, you might find it helpful to refer to them.

So Then, Just as You Received Christ Jesus

1. Based on your knowledge of the Bible, how does a person "receive" Jesus Christ? Give verses to support your answer.

2. How did you come to receive Christ? Everybody's story is unique. On page 84 write a brief outline of how you became a Christian. Include a few indications of the difference Christ makes in you now. (This will be particularly important if you have been a Christian from childhood.) Prepare your story in such a way that you could tell it to a nonChristian friend. Here are a few hints:

   a. Keep it short. You should be able to tell the essential details in 3 to 4 minutes.
   b. Make it personal. You are not preaching; you are recounting your personal experience.
   c. Keep Christ central. There's no need to dwell on your past. Neither do you want to emphasize how wonderful you are now. Focus on what Christ has done for you, and on some specific ways in which He has changed you.
   d. Avoid jargon. You've probably already picked up Christian phrases like "receive Christ." Think of ways of expressing what you mean in everyday language.
   e. Use the Bible. Adding a verse of Scripture that is relevant (perhaps one you have memorized) can give added impact.

Once you have prepared your testimony, tell it to another Christian and ask him to comment on its clarity. Then make a list of three or more nonChristian friends you would like to tell about your experience with Christ. Start praying for opportunities.

Prayer list:

As Lord

3. Read Colossians 1:15-20, 2:9-10, and 2:15.

   a. Based on these verses, what does it mean to speak of Jesus Christ as Lord?

b. How important is it for our salvation that Jesus Christ is Lord?

There is powerful logic in these verses. Unless Christ is the Lord of the universe, He does not have the power and authority to save people. If we believe that He can save us, then we must believe that He is the Lord of the universe. And if He is, then we must acknowledge Him as Lord over our personal lives as well.

4. In your own words, express the idea, "You have received Christ Jesus as Lord."

Continue to Live in Him

5. Listed below and on page 86 are some of the responses involved in receiving Christ Jesus as Lord. Explain why each one needs to be a continuing feature of our Christian lives.

a. Learning about Christ, recognizing who He is, and what He has done for us

b. Repenting of our sinful attitudes and actions

c. Putting our faith in Him

d. Submitting to Him as Lord

"Happy is he who makes daily progress and who considers not what he did yesterday but what advance he can make today."

—JEROME*

ASK YOURSELF: a. Is there one area listed above in which I am not continuing as I should? **b.** What can I do to continue to make progress?

Rooted and Built Up in Him

In the original Greek, "rooted" is in the past tense, whereas "built up" is in the present tense. Just as we received Christ Jesus as Lord once for all time, and now need to continue to live in Him, so also we were rooted in Christ once for all time, and now need to be built up in Him.

Rooted . . . in Him

6. The picture of a Christian being "in Christ" is a favorite one that the Apostle Paul uses often. One of the most striking passages is Ephesians 1:3-14.

    a. According to verse 13, how does a person come to be "in Christ"?

    b. In the passage, what are some of the benefits of being in Christ?

Note: Second Corinthians 5:17 includes the amazing statement that "if anyone is in Christ, he is a new creation." The meaning of this is explored in lesson 1 of *Living by His Grace*.

Built Up in Him

7. Read again Colossians 2:1-10, which provides context for verses 6 and 7.

    a. How would the Apostle Paul answer someone who said that to grow in the Christian life requires special knowledge over and above our knowledge of Christ?

b. How would he answer someone who said that there is a fullness needed for Christian living over and above what we have in Christ?

The Wheel illustration is a helpful way to remember the centrality of Christ in Christian growth. It also highlights the basic elements of a growing Christian life.

The Christian is represented by the rim of the wheel—in daily contact with the world. But the Christian life in the world draws its purpose, power, and direction from Christ, the Hub of the wheel. Smooth and steady progress is possible only as long as Christ remains central. The spokes of the wheel represent practical ways in which we can ensure that Christ stays at the center of our lives. God, by His Spirit, breathes into these activities and uses them to deepen our relationship with Christ.

In terms of God's provision, there are no barriers to growth. He has given us everything we need, for He has given us Himself. Whatever God requires of us, we can do because we are in Christ. Developing as a Christian involves entering into a deeper awareness of our riches in Christ, and learning to appropriate His resources on a daily basis.

---

8. Read John 15:1-17, in which Jesus teaches His disciples how to maintain growing relationships with Himself. Compare the passage with the Wheel illustration on the previous page, and try to write an appropriate reference from John 15 on each part of the wheel.

For Further Study

The word *rooted* has the common meaning of being planted. It can also be used to describe the laying of a foundation for a building. Paul develops both these pictures in 1 Corinthians 3:5-17. What can you learn about Christian growth from this passage?

Strengthened in the Faith as You Were Taught, and Overflowing with Thankfulness.

THE FAITH: *The faith* is to be distinguished from *faith*. Faith is an attitude of reliance on God. The faith is the body of Christian belief. It is the apostolic teaching and preaching given to the Church once and for all. This teaching is recorded in the New Testament and forms the authoritative standard for the Church's faith and practice in every age.

Note: This theme is developed in lesson 4 of *Living by His Grace*.

Strengthened in the Faith as You Were Taught

9. According to Ephesians 4:11-16, how can other believers help us become stronger in the faith?

10. a. What warning did Paul give the church leaders in Acts 20:28-32?

b. How can we be protected against false teaching?

Overflowing with Thankfulness

11. Thankfulness is an important part of Christian living. For example, look at Colossians 3:15-17. The phrase *overflowing with thankfulness* suggests that increased understanding of the Christian faith should lead to increased thankfulness. As you look back over the truths you studied in this book, which ones excited you the most and prompted you to express thanks to God?

Why not pause right now and thank God for these truths?

> **ASK YOURSELF:** What can I do to deepen my grasp of the faith?

Stop, Think, and Pray

After completing a lesson like this, it is tempting to try to put a lot of good intentions into practice at once. You may have learned a number of new things, but it is important to focus on one and put it into practice. Ask God to show you what it should be—what He wants you to do as a result of this lesson.

The response God is asking me to make

The action I should take

REMEMBER

Suggested memory verse for the question, What now?

So then, just as you received Christ Jesus as Lord,
continue to live in him, rooted and built up in him,
strengthened in the faith as you were taught, and
overflowing with thankfulness. (Colossians 2:6-7)

Your Response

In your study of lesson 1, you may have become aware that you have never truly reponded to the Christian gospel. The following is a simple outline of how you can make that response.

Step One: You must recognize your need.

- "God created man in his own image" (Genesis 1:27). As human beings, we are unique, with special capabilities and special responsibilities.
- God intends that we should live our lives in intimate relationship with Him, thus providing us with direction to live life to the full.
- But part of our humanity is the freedom to choose, to make moral decisions. That freedom is often exercised in the wrong way. Man chooses to rebel, to go his own way.
- The result is that man's original intimate relationship with God is broken. We are rebels rather than loyal subjects. Our lives are less than God intends them to be. And the image of God is marred and distorted.
- Because of moral wrongdoing, every one of us is in a predicament: we are separated from God's presence (Isaiah 59:1-2, Colossians 1:21); we fall short of God's standard (Isaiah 53:6, Romans 3:23); we deserve God's judgment (Ephesians 2:3, 2 Thessalonians 1:8-9); we are incapable of rescuing ourselves (Romans 5:8, Ephesians 2:1).

Step Two: You must accept what Jesus Christ has done.
- Jesus Christ demonstrates what man could be like. He is "full of grace and truth" (John 1:14), a perfect Man, "tempted in every way, just as we are—yet . . . without sin" (Hebrews 4:15).
- As Man, He stood in our place and took upon Himself the consequences of our wrongdoing. He suffered on the cross the judgment we deserved: "Christ died for sins once for all, the righteous for the unrighteous, to bring you to God" (1 Peter 3:18).
- But Jesus Christ is not just Man. He is God become Man: "For in Christ all the fullness of the Deity lives in bodily form" (Colossians 2:9). The Cross was God's plan: "God was reconciling the world to himself in Christ" (2 Corinthians 5:19).
- The uniqueness of Christ's Person is seen in His victory over death. He was crucified, dead, and buried, but on the third day He rose from the dead, demonstrating the completion of His work. He took the judgment for sin. He suffered the agony of death. But sin and death could not overcome Him. He rose triumphant and He lives forever. He has opened up for us the possibility of new life.

Step Three: You must respond personally to Christ.
- "Repent and believe the good news!" (Mark 1:15).
- We repent by acknowledging our wrongdoing before God. We have fallen short of His standards. We have resisted His rule over our lives. We may not have the strength to put right those things in our lives that are wrong, but we must be willing to let them go with God's help.
- We believe by putting our trust in what Christ has done on the cross as the only basis for our acceptance with God. "He saved us, not because of righteous things we had done, but because of his mercy" (Titus 3:5). We demonstrate our faith in Christ by opening up our lives to Him and inviting His Spirit to come and live within us. Jesus said, "Here I am! I stand at the door and knock. If anyone hears my voice and opens the door, I will go in and eat with him, and he with me" (Revelation 3:20).
- Here is a prayer that you could make your own. Before you pray, be quiet and realize that the living Christ is with you.

Lord Jesus Christ, I admit that I have sinned and gone my own way. I need Your forgiveness. I am willing to turn away from all that I know is wrong. I want to live with You. I want You to be first in my life. Thank You for dying on the cross to take away my sins. Thank You for Your gift of forgiveness and new life. I now take Your gift. I ask You to come into my life by Your Holy Spirit. Come in to fill my life. Come in as my Savior and Lord. Come in to be with me forever.
Thank You, Lord Jesus. Amen.

- If you have genuinely prayed, believe that Christ has heard you and answered you. Don't depend on your feelings. Trust the promise of Christ and quietly thank Him that He is now with you by His Spirit and has promised never to leave you.

And Now

- You have a new life: "God has given us eternal life, and this life is in his Son. He who has the Son has life; he who does not have the Son of God does not have life" (1 John 5:11-12).
- You have a new status: "To all who received him [Jesus], to those who believed in his name, he gave the right to become children of God" (John 1:12).
- You are a new person: "Therefore, if anyone is in Christ, he is a new creation; the old has gone, the new has come!" (2 Corinthians 5:17).

Rest secure in your new life. Take advantage of your privileged position as a child of God and talk to Him often in prayer. Recognize that becoming a new person is just the beginning. Now you can grow up into the person God wants you to be. The other studies in this *Learning to Live* series will help you discover how. You should also seek out other Christians who can help you and encourage you in your new life.

Memorizing Scripture

As You Start to Memorize a Verse

1. Read in your Bible the context of each verse you memorize.
2. Try to gain a clear understanding of what each verse actually means. (You may want to read the verse in other Bible translations or paraphrases to get a better grasp of the meaning.)
3. Read the verse several times thoughtfully, aloud or in a whisper. This will help you grasp the verse as a whole. Each time you read it, say the topic, reference, verse, and then the reference again.
4. Discuss the verse with God in prayer, and continue to seek His help for success in Scripture memory.

While You Are Memorizing a Verse

5. Work on saying the verse aloud as much as possible.
6. Learn the topic and reference first.
7. After learning the topic and reference, learn the first phrase of the verse. Once you have learned the topic, reference, and first phrase and have repeated them several times, continue adding more phrases, one at a time.
8. Think about how the verse applies to you and your daily circumstances.
9. Always include the topic and reference as part of the verse as you learn it and review it.

After You Have Memorized a Verse

10. Write the verse from memory and check your accuracy. This deepens the impression in your mind.
11. Review the verse immediately after learning it, and repeat it frequently in the next few days. This is crucial for getting the verse firmly fixed in your mind, because of how quickly we tend to forget what we have recently learned.
12. REVIEW! REVIEW! REVIEW! Repetition is the best way to engrave the verse on your memory.

Who's Who

Below, listed in alphabetical order, are brief biographical sketches of the figures from the history of the Church who are quoted in this Bible study.

Athanasius (295-373)
Bishop of Alexandria from 328. He was a staunch defender of the orthodox doctrine of the Person of Christ in opposition to Arianism. His steadfastness, which resulted in five periods of exile, was instrumental in saving the Church from this heresy.

Baxter, Richard (1615-1691)
English Puritan preacher and pastor who, because of his reformed views, was forced out of the Church of England and later imprisoned in the Tower for eighteen months. He wrote more than one hundred books, including *The Saint's Everlasting Rest, The Reformed Pastor,* and *A Call to the Unconverted.*

Jerome (347-420)
Roman theologian and monk. He was the leading scholar of his time, and his revision of the Latin text of the Bible (the Vulgate) became the standard Latin Bible.

Lewis, C.S. (1898-1963)
English novelist, poet, and author. He was converted to Christ while a lecturer at Oxford University. He went on to become

Professor of Medieval and Renaissance English Literature at Cambridge, a popular defender of the Christian faith, and "apostle to the sceptics." He wrote a number of works on theology and fantasy, including such classics as *The Screwtape Letters* and *The Chronicles of Narnia*.

Livingstone, David (1813-1873)
Scottish missionary and explorer. He established mission stations in remote parts of South Africa, and discovered such natural wonders as the Victoria Falls. He was also concerned about eradicating slave trading.

Luther, Martin (1483-1546)
The son of a German peasant, who came to a dynamic understanding of justification by faith while studying Romans and Galatians as a monk. In 1517 he challenged the corruption in the Church of his day, nailing his famous "Ninety-five Theses" to the church door in Wittenburg. The response of the Church eventually led to the Reformation, and the establishment of the Protestant church. Luther also translated the New Testament into German.

Origen (185-254)
Born in Alexandria, Egypt, of Christian parents. His father was martyred in 202, and Origen was restrained from following him only by his mother hiding his clothes! He was appointed to instruct candidates for baptism while in his teens and went on to become a famous Bible scholar, teacher, and writer.

Spurgeon, Charles (1834-1892)
Victorian Baptist renowned for his direct and powerful preaching. Before he was twenty years old, he became pastor of New Park Street Chapel in London and soon drew vast crowds. The six thousand-seat Metropolitan Tabernacle was erected, and Spurgeon preached there regularly for thirty years. He also founded a college for pastors.

Temple, William (1881-1944)
Archbishop of Canterbury, particularly noted for his concern for Christian unity and for a just society.

Wesley, Charles (1708-1788)
The great hymn writer of the English evangelical revival. In
over six thousand hymns, he captured the message of his
brother John and other leaders like George Whitefield.

Wesley, John (1703-1791)
A great preacher of the English evangelical revival. Although
already a Church of England minister, he came to a living faith
in 1738. Prevented from speaking in churches, he traveled
more than 250,000 miles and preached at least 40,000 sermons,
mainly in the open air. He organized the converts into classes
and societies, which developed into the Methodist Church
after his death.

For Further Reading

1. What Is the Gospel?

Blanchard, John, *Right with God*, Moody Press
Green, Michael, *Evangelism in the Early Church*, Eerdmans
    Publishing Company
Stott, John, *Basic Christianity*, InterVarsity Press
Stott, John, *Becoming a Christian* (booklet), InterVarsity Press

2. Who Is Jesus?

Anderson, J.N.D., *Evidence for the Resurrection*, InterVarsity
    Press
McDonald, H. Dermont, *Jesus—Human and Divine*, Baker
    Book House
McDowell, Josh, *Evidence that Demands a Verdict*, Here's Life
    Publishers
Milne, Bruce, *Know the Truth*, InterVarsity Press

3. Why the Cross?

Lloyd-Jones, David M., *Romans*, volume 1, Zondervan Publish-
    ing House
Milne, Bruce, *Know the Truth*, InterVarsity Press
Morris, Leon, *The Cross in the New Testament*, Eerdmans
    Publishing Company

4. What Is a Christian?

Packer, J.I., *God's Words*, InterVarsity Press

Packer, J.I., *Knowing God*, InterVarsity Press
Stott, John, *Being a Christian* (booklet), InterVarsity Press

5. Can We Be Sure?

Lloyd-Jones, David M., *Romans*, volume 2, Zondervan Publishing House

6. What Now?

Eims, LeRoy, *What Every Christian Should Know about Growing*, Victor Books/Scripture Press
Shallis, Ralph, *From Now On*, STL Books